Community Workers

Taking You Places

A Book About Bus Drivers

Ann Owen

Illustrated by Eric Thomas

Thanks to our advisers for their expertise, research, knowledge, and advice:

Michael Setzer, General Manager, Metro Transit, Minneapolis, Minnesota

Susan Kesselring, M.A., Literacy Educator Rosemount-Apple Valley-Eagan (Minnesota) School District

PICTURE WINDOW BOOKS
Minneapolis, Minnesota

Managing Editor: Bob Temple
Creative Director: Terri Foley
Editor: Peggy Henrikson
Editorial Adviser: Andrea Cascardi
Copy Editor: Laurie Kahn
Designer: John Moldstad
Page production: Picture Window Books
The illustrations in this book were prepared digitally.

Picture Window Books
1710 Roe Crest Drive
North Mankato, MN 56003
www.capstonepub.com

Library of Congress Cataloging-in-Publication Data
Owen, Ann, 1953–
Taking you places : a book about bus drivers / written by Ann Owen ; illustrated by Eric Thomas.
p. cm. — (Community workers)
Summary: Describes some of the things that bus drivers do to help people get where they need to go.
Includes bibliographical references and index.
ISBN 978-1-4048-0090-8 (hardcover)
ISBN 978-1-4048-0484-5 (paperback)
1. Bus drivers—Juvenile literature. 2. Community life—Juvenile literature. 3. Bus lines—Juvenile literature.
[1. Bus drivers. 2. Occupations.] I. Thomas, Eric, ill. II. Title. III. Community workers (Picture Window Books)
TL232.3 .O94 2004
388.3'22044'023—dc21
                                                                                    2003004216

Many people
in your community
have jobs helping others.

What do bus drivers do?

The school bus driver starts your school day.

5

The bus driver makes sure you are safe.

Please sit down.

The bus driver stops at railroad tracks.

The bus driver stops traffic.

The bus driver makes sure
you get to school on time.

Sometimes the bus driver takes you on field trips

to the fire station,

a museum,

or maybe the zoo.

Some bus drivers drive city buses.

They take you downtown,

to the mall,

or even to the library.

A bus driver follows a schedule
and picks you up on time.

The bus driver helps you find places.

Other bus drivers can take you far away

and bring you back home again.

Bus drivers take you places.

Did You Know?

- A bus driver must get a special driver's license. The driver needs to know the laws and safety rules of driving his or her kind of bus and the schedule and route to follow. School bus drivers need to know first aid, what to do in an emergency, and how to help children who have special needs. They also need to know school rules. City bus drivers and city-to-city bus drivers need to learn how to figure fares and how to work well with passengers. They have to write reports on their trips as well as on the care of their buses.

- School buses are the safest way to travel. Riding a school bus is safer than traveling on an airplane, in a car, or on a passenger train.

- City buses now have special places for wheelchair users to clamp and belt in their wheelchairs for a safe ride. Some city buses have bike racks on the front.

- The first bus was invented more than 300 years ago in France. It carried eight people and was pulled by horses. The first gas-powered bus was invented in Germany more than 100 years ago.

- The first city in the United States to have a bus service was New York City. This service began in 1830, about 175 years ago. Buses still were pulled by horses. They often carried passengers both inside the bus and on the roof.

Kinds of Buses

Buses take you places near and far. A bus driver usually specializes in driving a certain kind of bus. This chart tells you about different kinds of buses.

Kind of Bus	What It Does	A Special Feature
School Bus	Takes children to and from school	Stop sign that comes out from the side to stop traffic
City Bus	Takes people to work, play, and shop around the city	A cord to pull or button to push when you want the bus driver to stop at the next stop
City-to-City Bus	Takes people from city to city around the country	A bathroom (and sometimes TVs and VCRs)
Motorcoach	Takes people on special tours	Comfortable seats, often on a higher level than the driver's seat

Words to Know

community (kuh-MYOO-nuh-tee)—a group of people who live in the same area

emergency (i-MUR-juhn-see)—something bad or dangerous that happens
and has to be handled quickly and right away

fare (FAIR)—the cost of riding the bus

passenger (PASS-uhn-jur)—someone besides the driver who rides in a vehicle

route (ROUT)—a particular way to go or series of places to stop

schedule (SKEJ-ool)—a plan for what to do and when to do it.
A bus driver's schedule tells the driver when to make each stop.

To Learn More

Flanagan, Alice K. Riding the School Bus with Mrs. Kramer. New York: Children's Press, 1998.

Gorman, Jacqueline Laks. Bus Driver. Milwaukee, Wis.: Weekly Reader Early Learning Library, 2002.

Klingel, Cynthia Fitterer. School Buses. Chanhassen, Minn.: Child's World, 2001.

Ready, Dee. School Bus Drivers. Mankato, Minn.: Bridgestone Books, 1998.

Wilson, Anthony. On the Move: A Visual Timeline of Transportation. New York: Dorling Kindersley, 1995.

Index